The Voices Project 2013:
Out of Place

The Market Brolosopher by Arda Barut
Untouchable by Tania Cañas
Birdcage by Christopher Harley
This Feral Life by Julia-Rose Lewis
The Mangroves by Tom Mesker
These Things Happen by Joel Perlgut
Silo by Charles Purcell
Peach by Isobel Roberts-Orr
Private Research by Randa Sayed
Sunrise Set by Krystal Sweedman
Falling Through the Blue/Grey by Sara West
Red Panda by Amanda Yeo

50 years YOUNG

australian
theatre for
young people

CURRENCY PRESS
SYDNEY

CURRENCY PLAYS

First published in 2013
by Currency Press Pty Ltd
PO Box 2287 Strawberry Hills NSW 2012
enquiries@currency.com.au
www.currency.com.au

NATIONAL LIBRARY OF AUSTRALIA CIP DATA

    Author: Barut, Arda.
    Title: The voices project 2013 : out of place / Arda Barut ... [et al.].
    ISBN: 9780868199788 (pbk.)
    Series: Voices project
    Subjects: Australian drama—21st century.
    Other Authors/Contributors:
                      Australian Theatre for Young People.
    Dewey Number: A822.4

Typeset by Katy Wall and Paul O'Beirne for Currency Press.
Cover design by Katy Wall for Currency Press.

This publication was supported by the Copyright
Agency Limited Cultural Fund and the Graeme
Wood Foundation

Currency Press acknowledges the Traditional Owners of the Country on which we live and
work. We pay our respects to all Aboriginal and Torres Strait Islander Elders, past and present.

Contents

Out of Place

DAN PRICHARD is the manager of **atyp**'s Fresh Ink new writing program and is the producer of *The Voices Project*. Originally from the UK, Dan has taught English in the Czech Republic, Mexico and Singapore, where he joined the British Council as Director of Arts and oversaw programs in theatre, performance poetry, film, design and new writing. For **atyp**, he is also currently producing FRESH PERSPECTIVES, a series of in-depth interviews with leading Australian playwrights and theatremakers.

Out of Place: Introduction
Dan Prichard

When we sat down to discuss the theme of this third collection of dramatic monologues for **atyp**'s *The Voices Project*, we were faced with a challenge: we'd covered love, we'd covered death—the BIG themes of anyone's life… so where could we possibly go from there?

But then, thinking back upon the conversations we'd had with our writers over the past two years, as our writers built their characters and their individual narratives, we realised the same questions kept coming up time and time again: Where are we from? What does it mean to belong and to find a place in the world? And where are we heading in our lives? Indeed, very often the characters of our previous stage shows grappled with these questions as much as they did with the ideas of love and parting, while the resulting monologues were so rich with a sense of a particular environment or landscape that they became almost palpable. So it wasn't such a huge leap for us to gravitate towards the idea of place and how it relates to identity as a ripe subject for this edition, and to set ourselves the task of dissecting the very notion of place as it applies to contemporary Australian teenage life.

In this, we were incredibly fortunate to have as the backdrop for the annual writing Studio, where *The Voices Project* monologues are first imagined, the extraordinary landscape of the Riversdale writers retreat at Bundanon, just outside Nowra in New South Wales. You'd be hard pressed to find a better place to contemplate the effect that environment can have on the soul. The centre was set up specifically to allow artists to step out of the frustrations and pressures of everyday life, and find themselves, each other and the physical and mental space to write. It's one of the delights of running Fresh Ink to witness the dazzled expressions on the faces of our writers when they see the valley for the first time.

Over the week spent at the centre developing the *Out of Place* monologues, mentored by leading Australian playwrights Lachlan Philpott, Ross Mueller and Vanessa Bates, and the UK's Ola Animashawun, our twenty writers from all over Australia examined what it means to be Australian in the 21st century, how that idea of nationhood is changing and what that means for Australian writers who are striving to find both their own voice and to articulate Australian stories.

We travelled from the quarries of outback Australia, to small country towns, from the markets of Flemington and Victoria to the bedrooms of Western Sydney. Iconic places were noticeably absent in this pyschogeography of another Australia, and even physical spaces gave way as 'place' often became something intangible, something to be found in friendships, a community of shared interest and in virtual online relationships. The claustrophobia of small town life compared and contrasted with the empty loneliness of the big cities; second generation Australians found themselves struggling with dual identity at the nexus of tradition, cultural memory and family expectations; while questions of history, class, race, religion and sexuality were all interrogated as the *Out of Place* characters emerged and began to find their voice.

And so here we are: twelve Australian stories, told by twelve young writers, through twelve beautifully realised characters. But there are many more stories to tell, many more Australias to be revealed. We hope you will join us in this journey of discovery.

Now, meet Abe, Tania, Lewis, Mia, Alison, Quinn, Tyson, El, Marwer, Sarah, Grem and Asmara.

Dan Prichard
Fresh Ink Manager
www.freshink.com.au

The twelve pieces in this publication are accompanied by essays on the monologue form by actor Luke Mullins, playwright Caleb Lewis and theatre and film director Laura Scrivano. You can find more such articles and more about *The Voices Project* on the Fresh Ink website, which also features interviews with leading playwrights, blog pieces, and information about the National Studio and other opportunities for working with us. Visit www.freshink.com.au

LUKE MULLINS is an actor, theatre-maker, director and dramaturg, who works extensively across the theatre sector. As a core member of Stuck Pigs Squealing he has been a creator and performer on *4xBeckett, Agoraphobe, The Eisteddfod, Lally Katz and the Terrible Mysteries of the Volcano, Untitled Intentional Exercise #1, Nine Days Falling* and co-directed and performed in Stuck Pigs' *The Apocalypse Bear Trilogy*, presented by the MTC and Melbourne Festival.

Luke was a member of the STC Actors Company and has worked extensively as an actor for Sydney Theatre Company, Melbourne Theatre Company, Malthouse Theatre and Belvoir. He has created and performed work with a number of independent companies including Uncle Semolina and Friends, Liminal, Uninvited Guests, Little Death, Wrecked all Prods and Arts Radar.

His independent practice includes *Autobiography of Red*, a solo work he created and performed for Malthouse Theatre and *Irony is not Enough: Essay on my Life as Catherine Deneuve* created with Fragment 31 at Arts House Melbourne. He performed the acclaimed solo work *Thom Pain (based on nothing)* at Downstairs Belvoir, directed by Sam Strong.

Luke has been awarded the George Fairfax Award for Excellence in Theatre Practice and a Green Room Award for *The Season at Sarsaparilla*.

Advice for Actors: Alone at Last

Luke Mullins

A solo monologue presents unique challenges, and each one will have its individual nuances depending on the requirements of the text. This is compounded by the fact there is no other actor to look to for support, inspiration, energy and help when things get off track.

Performing a monologue can also be an incredibly liberating and empowering experience. With nowhere to hide, you are forced to come right to the front of yourself as a performer. You have ownership of interpretation, and control over exactly where you want to go moment-to-moment in performance, exploring different possibilities and allowing yourself to be surprised by the outcome.

Here are a few things to consider when performing a solo monologue:

1. Know who you are speaking to

Another character

If you're speaking to a character who is not being played onstage by another actor, have a definite sense of where they're located. Resist planting yourself and staring at eye level about two metres in front of you into the face of an imaginary person. This will only undermine your ability to create the imagined reality of the piece for yourself and for the audience. There are a huge range of things people do when talking to each other. Eyeballing for a length of time is rarely one.

Rather than being concerned about the physical absence of the character you're talking to, focus instead on your relationship to this person. Be absolutely clear how you feel about them and why you're speaking to them. What do you need from the other person? What are you trying to do to them? If you're detailed and specific about what you're *doing* and what you're *reacting to* moment-to-moment, then where to look will be revealed to you.

The audience

Speaking directly to the audience can be confronting, but it can also liberate you from having to construct and maintain an imagined reality all by yourself. You can view the audience as the character you're speaking to or just as themselves: a group of people who have come to listen to what you have to say.

In his monologue play *Thom Pain (based on nothing)*, writer Will Eno lists the Dramatis Personae as 'Thom Pain' and 'Audience'. Acknowledging the audience's presence and talking directly to them creates a shift in the relationship and transaction taking place. The audience becomes part of the story—another character, and must now be treated as such.

You can apply the same principles to the audience as you would another character—but you can't rehearse their response! Be alive to the large and subtle differences every night and adjust to what they bring as the other character in your play. Being able to ride their responses and respond authentically in the moment will be key to making your piece work.

Yourself

Soliloquy is talking to yourself when you are alone onstage, without directly addressing the audience. It often reveals the character's thoughts and feelings or is a way for a character to work through an idea or a problem for themselves. Hamlet is the clearest example of this; there are many moments alone onstage where he sorts through his thoughts, weighs up his options and tries to spur himself into action. The risk with addressing a monologue to yourself is that it can become reflective and passive. To ensure it is active, use actions to activate the text but address them to yourself: 'I command myself', 'I console myself', 'I berate myself'.

2. Being present

Performing alone requires you to be present in a very particular way. Often onstage actors are either striving forward, pushing for what they think the performance should be; or they are falling back into themselves in an attempt to be authentic. Both will take you away from being present. This is especially important to remember in solo performance as you don't have another actor to connect with, anchoring you in the reality of what is going on in the moment. Don't get lost in yourself or what you're trying to do. Always be alert to what is happening right now in this room between you and the audience.

3. Storytelling

Often in monologues an actor is required to tell a story in a more literal way. It could be something from the past, a memory, or something that happened to someone else. Don't fall into the trap of just 'telling a story' or recounting an event, lapsing into the past or into a memory. Always focus on why this is being said in the present. Why are you telling this story *in this moment* to someone else, to the audience or to yourself? What do you need to do to them now and how are you using this story to do it?

In scene four of *The Glass Menagerie* Tom comes home drunk at five in the morning and tells his sister Laura where he's been and what he's been doing. Rather than 'recounting the story' of his evening (passive and in the past) he is actually trying to evade her questions, escape the truth of the night's events, and distract her with an onslaught of detail (active and in the present). Always look for why the story is being told and play *that*, rather than simply relaying the story itself.

4. Serve the text

Understand the writer's intention. Get the words right and let us hear them. Observe the punctuation. Don't impose anything on it that it doesn't need. Observe the stage directions: if they're good they will ignite your imagination rather than close it down. Don't demonstrate the text: if you are *saying* it, don't *do* it. The actor's job is to bring inner life and new layers of meaning to the writing, so don't 'act it out' for us—reveal what it means to you.

5. It is not a solo

Although you may be the only person onstage you are not working alone: the light and the shadow, the sound and the silence, the space and the theatre, the audience and the text. These things will give you excellent material to respond to, allowing you to be affected and changed. Giving attention to them will keep you in the present moment.

6. It is not a monologue

In life, unless giving a lecture or a formal speech, no one begins speaking knowing that they will speak uninterrupted for one, ten, or thirty minutes. Approach your piece as a scene where the other person / the audience doesn't get a chance to reply, or doesn't choose to speak. Pause for a response from the other character, from the audience or for yourself to consider what you have said. Cut off the other person. Prevent them from responding. Wonder what they are going to say. Be affected and changed by what they do or do not say and do. Find the need to speak the next line.

7. Put it outside yourself

Do not disappear inside yourself when performing alone. There is no one else to draw you out and no one else for the audience to connect to, so you are effectively giving them permission to shut off. Always place what it is you want, your intention, outside yourself. Put it on the other person, the audience, an imagined person, place or object.

8. Don't forget the basics

As always these fundamentals will help you out of trouble:

- Create clear, simple objectives and tasks for yourself so that you are always active and moving forward.

- Use transitive verbs, i.e., verbs that can be done to someone or something, 'I accuse you', 'I tease you', 'I caress the book', 'I study the ceiling'. Avoid all forms of the verb 'to be' such as 'being elated' or 'being angry'.

- Avoid generalisations and states of being. 'I am sad', 'The character is very depressed', 'I am full of rage'. None of these are things you can actually *do.* They are non-specific and won't help you to be active onstage.

Hopefully these few pointers will be helpful to come back to—especially when things seem complicated. Don't fall back to ways of doing it that you have set in stone—the more rigid you are, the more likely to break under stress. The structure with some give—that retains its shape but can bend to accommodate any weather—will be the one that stays standing in the end. Enjoy your opportunity to have such a personal relationship to an audience. Prepare well, and once you step onstage all you have to do is be present and find the need to speak.

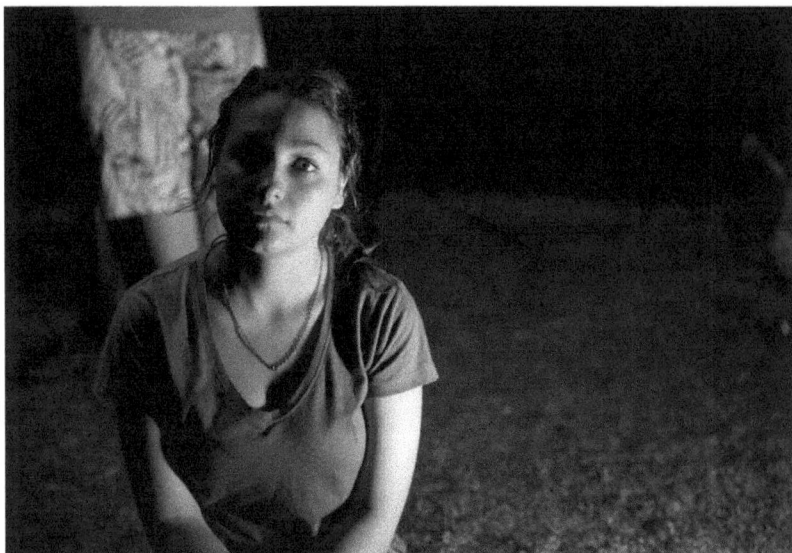

Sophie Irvine in atyp's Tell it Like it Isn't, 2011 (photo Alex Vaughan)

Rosie Connolly in atyp's Tell it Like it Isn't, 2011 (photo Alex Vaughan)

Rhys Keir in atyp's The One Sure Thing, 2012 (photo Olivia Martin-McGuire)

Emma Campbell in atyp's The One Sure Thing, 2012 (photo Olivia Martin-McGuire)

CALEB LEWIS is a multi-award-winning playwright, produced locally and overseas. He has twice been shortlisted for the Griffin Award and is the winner of an Inscription Award, the Mitch Mathews Award and an AWGIE (Australian Writer's Guild Award). His plays include *Nailed, Dogfall, Crystal, The Sea Bride, Songs for the Deaf, Men, Love & the Monkeyboy, Death in Bowengabbie, Rust and Bone, Aleksander and the Robot Maid* and *Clinchfield*. Other entertainments include *From the Outside Looking In* and *Across a Crowded Room*. Current projects include commissions for Bell Shakespeare, Onward Productions, State Theatre Company South Australia and SBS Television. In 2011 *Rust and Bone* was one of four plays showcased at PlayWriting Australia's National Play Festival. The play premieres at Griffin Theatre in 2013, the same year his latest play *Maggie Stone*, debuts at STCSA. Lewis is also the inaugural winner of the Richard Burton New Play Award, for his play, *Clinchfield*. Caleb was one of the 2011 National Studio tutors, along with Peta Murray and Ross Mueller. A selection of works that resulted were performed in *The Voices Project 2012: The One Sure Thing* in February 2012 and published by Currency Press that year.

Advice for Writers:
On Writing Monologues
Caleb Lewis

There are few moments onstage more powerful than a good monologue. Done right it's an act of virtuosity, a brief moment of stillness where everything else falls away save one startling single voice. Done badly it's a twenty-minute drum solo—at best self-indulgent, at worst an interruption the audience endures waiting patiently for the show to resume.

A great monologue might work for many reasons, but a dud usually falls over when it stumbles on one of the following. When writing your own monologue here are ten things to consider:

1. Speech, soliloquy and story

First off, who is your character talking to? If they are talking to another character (played by another actor onstage or by nobody or even by the audience) then it's a speech. Now we need to know a few things. Who is this other character? What is their relationship? This changes both the story and how it is told. You speak differently to your mother than you do to a stranger than you do to a child. Knowing who this other person is in your monologist's life will decide how much your character opens up to them, how familiar they already are and what kind of language they use.

If your character is talking to him- or herself it's a soliloquy. Is this an internal monologue the audience is privy to or are they rehearsing a speech for later? There's a difference.

Lastly your character may talk to the audience directly, as is the case for a narrator or Greek chorus. In this case they are often (though not always) telling us the story of someone else. Often (though not always) your narrator knows all. Often (though not always) they tell the story in third person, i.e., 'then Jack climbed the beanstalk, etc.' Here the storyteller's own identity is not the point. They are simply a tale teller and the means by which the story is told.

2. Who is this guy?

Who is doing the talking?

What does this person looks like? How are they dressed? How do they move? How do they speak? When people open their mouths they tell us so much more than simply what they're saying. Just by listening we can tell things like their gender, their nationality and their age. Do they speak plainly or with a silver tongue? Do they present clearly or repeat themselves often? Do they speak bluntly or seek reassurance with lots of questions? What vernacular they speak in might hint at their background*; what jargon they use might give away their occupation.

3. Motive

In drama as in life, characters only open their mouths if they want something. Speech without an intention is just bad exposition. What does your character want? Forgiveness? Help? Directions? Why are they telling us their dog died now? Are they trying to warn us about something? Are they consoling us by sharing their own private grief? Or are they buttering us up before they ask to borrow another hundred dollars? Each of these motives is different and each will affect the way the story is told.

4. Learn how to write silence

5. Stage directions

Less is more. If you enjoy writing detailed stage directions write a novel. Directors ignore them anyway. Rather, choose your battles. Decide which stage directions are vital and remove all the others. Those that remain will be considered more carefully. Concentrate on your job and let the actors do theirs. Give your cast space to explore. Never tell an actor how to deliver a line.

---

*Shakespeare's Othello was a naval commander and speaks often using maritime analogies.

6. Don't spell it out

David Mamet said, 'The job of the dramatist is to make the audience wonder what happens next, not to explain to them what just happened.'

Good writing raises questions and then rewards us with a partial answer. This in turn raises another question which will only be rewarded by continuing to watch. It keeps the audience intrigued and absorbed. Bad writing over-explains with an info dump. The writer doesn't trust his audience to figure the story out so he telegraphs the plot in skywriting overhead. Your audience isn't dumb. Trust them.

7. Suspense is your friend

Suspense is created by rousing the audience's curiosity, by posing questions and delaying answers, by creating bigger and bigger complications and delaying resolutions. Think about Ridley Scott's *Alien* or Spielberg's *Jaws*. For most of both films we never see the threat directly, instead we get glimpses and shadows, piquing our curiosity, tantalising us more and more, then finally rewarding us.

8 Poetry versus prose

Both are powerful. Know their place. Poetry is seductive but beware of overusing it. Next to the verbal dexterity and rich imagery of poetry, prose can feel like its simple plainer cousin. It may not be as pretty as poetry but prose is the language of action and nothing is as direct. When somebody's trapped in a burning building they don't scream, 'Look how these flickering flames dance like gaily coloured gypsies all around me!'. They scream, 'Help!'.

9. Subtext

What is not said is often far more interesting than what is spoken out loud. Think Edward Albee's *Who's Afraid of Virginia Woolf* or Henrik Ibsen's *Ghosts*. These people find it almost impossible to say what they want to say, instead they circle around topics endlessly talking about everything *but* whatever needs to be said. Subtext is the elephant in the room.

10. Truth and perspective

Lastly how much does your narrator know and how much do they think they know? Do they know the whole story or only a part of it?

What don't they know? What have they guessed? What have they got wrong? What might they have made up? What are they keeping back? What do they have to gain by telling us the truth? What do they have to gain by lying to us? And finally how do we know we can trust their word?

This list is by no means comprehensive but it's a good start. The monologue is a simple and effective device and one that every writer worth their salt should have a grip on.

Felix Dupuy in atyp's Tell it Like it Isn't, 2011 (photo Alex Vaughan)

Kyle McLeavey in atyp's Tell it Like it Isn't, 2011 (photo Alex Vaughan)

Laura Hopkinson in atyp's Tell it Like it Isn't, 2011 (photo Alex Vaughan)

Adam Marks in atyp's Tell it Like it Isn't, 2011 (photo Alex Vaughan)

LAURA SCRIVANO is a filmmaker, writer and theatre director of Italian-Australian heritage. Recent film credits include the short films *The Orchard*, *Ricochet* and *Hairpin*, which screened at national and international film festivals. Laura also directed the filmed monologues *Boot* and *Little Love* for *The Voices Project* in 2012, and is directing *The Language of Love* by Kim Ho and *RE:BOOT*, the online mash-up of the original *Boot* monologue, for *The Voices Project* in 2013. Recent theatre credits include *Polyopera* for Opera Australia, *Sweet Bird andsoforth* for Mess Hall/Under the Wharf and *Stories from an Invisible Town* for Hoipolloi, UK. Laura is the creative director of Mess Hall, a collective of artists producing film and theatre projects (facebook.com/messhallproductions) and tweets @ laurascrivano. Laura recently completed the full-time Graduate Diploma in Directing at AFTRS.

Advice for Directors:
The Space Between

Laura Scrivano

Writing is all about the words, right?

Words form the scaffolding around which we build our stories, the foundation stone of the transaction between the audience and the author. And in a dramatic monologue, they're essential.

But for me, as a director, story starts with character. And a character can be revealed as much by what they don't say, as what they do. Clever lines and pithy prose don't offer dramatic possibilities. I'm interested in the spaces between the words, the pauses, ellipses, breaks and breaths. While the words carry the meaning of the story, the spaces between reveal truth. They can make a character believable, empathetic and authentic, which are ultimately the reasons why an audience will invest in and be moved by a story.

The space between is where I started when I was asked to direct *Boot* and *Little Love* for *The Voices Project* in 2012. But, there were really two spaces between; those between the words and the space between theatre and cinematic storytelling that these stories would inhabit.

Filming a piece of writing originally penned for the theatre can be fraught with problems, especially when that piece is a monologue— an inherently theatrical form. Monologues exist rarely on film, and when they do it's often to alienate or shock the audience. And the brief for *The Voices Project* is to engage the audience with the writing and storytelling. Although the goal is inherently the same in both film and theatre—to tell a story that will move or connect with an audience— the theatrical form is a world away from cinematic storytelling. On film, the audience's experience is no longer live; the eye of the camera mediates and dictates their visual world, the performance rhythms, the story beats and ultimately their feeling states.

In essence we were creating something between theatre and film. We were expressing theatrical writing through the camera lens. Monologues can have 8–10 minutes worth of text—much more dialogue than would ever be in a filmed adaptation of the same story. The biggest challenge would be to keep the audience watching.

With *Boot* and *Little Love*, we achieved this by focusing on the performances, setting up a simple but strong *mise-en-scène* (the compositional elements in the frame) and finding an editing style that matched the emotional temperature of the stories. For example, I wanted the unstable, raw energy of *Boot* to sit alongside Laura Hopkinson's wonderful performance so we shot it outside, where she is exposed and alone, while the jump cut editing matches the inflections of her syntax and emotions as she re-lives the night of the accident. In *Little Love* I wanted to capture the surprising sensuality of Adam's lovemaking with Bat Eyes—hence the mirrored surfaces, water, breath and touch became prominent elements. Looking at the monologues filmed for 2013, other approaches are possible. When Stephen McCallum directed *Hunger* he used projections to visualise the emotions the character was experiencing at each stage of the monologue. Pre-filming the projection elements allowed Steve to create a striking visual world while giving actor Tom Stokes the freedom to find the journey of his character. Martha Goddard has focused on using the nuances of the writing in her interpretation of *Stick*, setting the scene for the character through sound design and performance.

When filming a monologue it's important to think about how the writing can be heightened, subtext created, or expectations subverted by performance, location, lighting and choice of shots. We shot *Boot* and *Little Love* with minimal lighting but even if you just have daylight at your disposal, the choice to shoot at sunrise or sunset or noon will have a dramatic impact on how the audience receives your story.

Keeping an audience engaged throughout a filmed monologue can be difficult. As cinemagoers we are used to economical storytelling, moving shots, fast paced editing and an orchestral score to keep us in our seats. Unless you're Steven Spielberg you probably don't have a large, professional film crew in your back pocket. So, here are some tips on how to make a monologue work on film:

Keep it short. Film can tell a story economically.

As a director, ask yourself: why is my character telling this story?

Who are they telling it to?

And why are they telling it now?

Your actor is your best tool. They are the conduits for your story—without them we wouldn't have a job! Learn to love your actor and the offers they bring to your writing, work with them collaboratively and be as clear as possible when communicating with them about their performance.

Shoot your actor at least three ways—wide shot, medium shot and close up. This gives you options in picking which take is best for performance and story.

Shoot some cutaways. You could do the whole monologue as a voiceover with other imagery or you could shoot cutaways of your actor's hands, eyes, the location, etc. Cutting to a new shot will visually refresh the audience, and can be used to heighten symbolism and metaphor in your story.

Music or underscoring can be extremely effective in heightening the drama. But make sure it's working for your story—there is nothing worse that the music dwarfing the writing or acting! Due to copyright make sure you use original music or music in the public domain. Check out the Creative Commons website for a selection of license-free music that you can use.

Trust your instincts. As a writer or director, you have great storytelling instincts, make sure you listen to them and fight for the story you want to tell.

Most importantly—have fun!

Enjoy creating your own filmed monologue—hopefully *The Voices Project* monologues go some way to providing insight into that space between, from which you can take an exhilarating leap into creative possibility.

Tom Stokes as Sam in atyp's filmed monologue *Hunger*, 2013 (photo Tim Barnsley)

Laura Hopkinson as Dana in atyp's filmed monologue *Boot*, 2012 (photo Laura Scrivano)

THE MARKET BROLOSOPHER
ARDA BARUT

Abe is a 16-year-old Lebanese teenager wearing tracksuit pants, a bum bag and a singlet, and has his side facing the audience as he tends to his stall at the market. The stage is set with two collapsible tables in front of and behind Abe that have shoes/camping bags and general camping gear on top. A camping stove is set out at the front of the stall.

ABE:

Abe calls out to the market.

Hey! Don't be a sook! Come have a look!

Pause.

Don't be a creep! It's very very cheap!

Pause.

Don't be a fag! Come buy a bag!

Abe sighs with boredom.

Fuck it's been a slow day bro.

Glances at the audience.

It's almost lunch and we've only made a hundred and sixty bucks. It's fucken dead bro. Fucken bullshit. My dad's gonna bust my balls at this rate. You know Bill Gates makes more money a minute then we make in a year bro? Fucken rich, white men.

He takes out a box of studded leather gloves and places them on display.

Look, I just got these in. They cost me an arm and a leg but we call sell 'em for forty a pair. They'll help us make six hundred by the end of the day. Don't tell my dad about them though,

26

it might get him in trouble with the stall manager— But don't worry bro, they're not knuckle busters or anything. Just leather gloves with metal studs. They're blunt. Just for show you know. For Vietnamese gangster wannabes.

Abe begins to put on a pair gloves.

Hey check this out bro.
Dhuk you.
Dhuk you madadaka, Dhuk you.

Abe turns himself completely towards the audience and repeats himself louder.

Dhuk yoouuu madddah dhukkkkaaa
Dhuk yoooooouuuuu
Ahy Kut you

He makes a slicing motion with his hands.

Kut you, Ahy Kut youuu
Dhukkk yoooouuuu

Abe turns back to the market as he notices a customer.

Oh shit.

He quickly removes his gloves and places them back in the box. He waits while the customer inspects the stove.

Nah this guy's wasting our time, he's just eyeing the stove—let me show you how it's done.

Abe resumes his Asian accent.

Ahy wewlkom you to mah store.

He holds up eight fingers.

That wan eiiyyttiii fayve dohlla—eiiyytiii fayve. Yeah. Baht for youuuu, I do eiiyttiii four dohllaa.

Pause. Customer leaves.

Window shoppers bro, you gotta get rid of 'em as quickly as possible. If we can get eighty-five for this stove we'll be alright. But we need to make a sale, we're not gonna get paid at this rate bro.

I promised I'd go watch *Avatar* with Ozzy tomorrow. Have you seen the trailer? The CGI is amazing. See Osman thinks the movie's good, I'm just going for the visuals. Whuhuyet Allah. They say it's the biggest leap in CGI technology since *The Matrix*. I swear.

Police approaching—

Remember that night when we were kids and my Dad took us out to watch *The Matrix* after we helped him shovel dirt in the back yard during Ramadan? He was pretty proud of us aye? That was a good night bro. Hey watch out for these cops, just throw something— throw that bag over the box of gloves.

Do it casually you gronk!

Long pause—Silence as Policemen walk by. Glances at audience.

Hey, watch this.

Out to Policemen.

You in the blue! Come buy a shoe!

He scoffs and faces the audience.

Pigs.

Pause.

You should come with us. I'm picking up Osman after work. He thinks he's king shit now because he got promoted. Bro, you know what he told me yesterday? He was telling me that Macca's is good 'cause it gives to charity. I told him it's worse that it gives to charity because it makes people like him *think* Maccas is good. See that's why I like Hungry Jacks. I mean—

Customer 2 Approaching—

It's like yep. You crave our burgers and we're gonna exploit that. None of this give-to-charity-with-one-hand-and-make-the-populace-obese-with-the-other, George Soros bullshit. At least when you have a whopper you feel guilty—
Selamin Aleykum!
Eighty-five for the stove brother, yeah that one's eighty-five. Good Quality.
No brother I can't. Eighty-five.
I can't.

Pause. Customer about to leave.

Hey, hey. Come here.

Pause.

Seventy-five.

Brother I told you I can't for that much. Seventy-five, that's the last price.
Yeah look we pack up by four—but it might be gone by then brother—it's the last one I have.
Okay, have a look, but come back later alright?

Long pause. Turns to audience.

It's the same shit with Harmony day. It should be called not-feeling-guilty-about-our-white-privilege day. That's the thing about multiculturalism. It's like fuck off, I don't want your toleration. I'm either an Australian or I'm not.

Customer 3 approaches and inspects bag covering studded gloves.

Don't patronise me with your 'oh you're from a different ethnic background so this is the special day we tolerate you and your people'. No. I don't tolerate your toleration.
Fiiifteeen dollah boss—This one goot—wery goot this one! Beckpek wih doubow zippa!
It's colonisation bro. I'm not joking. Yeah you come to Lakemba,

eat our hummus and falafel, but when you see someone in a hijab that's not alright—

Takes the bag off the box of studded gloves to show Customer 3.

Hey boss, hey, come, for you I do ten dolla? Hey pwease, wery cheap!

Sighs, puts bag on a table to his side.

Stingy Asians bro. If we can get rid of a few of these gloves we'll be alright.

Customer 4 approaches and analyses the stove.

Pause.

He whispers to audience.

Hey this Aussie looks like he knows what he wants bro.

Abe takes on an Anglo-Australian accent.

How ya goin? The stoves nighty-five mate. That's good quality. Heavy duty stuff right there. Last one I got.

Whaddya need it for?

Oh yeah?

Listen, I sell this stove to two types of people. Guys like you who want it for a barby, and fat Lebanese mothers with fifteen kids. Look I'll be honest, what's it worth to ya?
It's yours for eighty-five.
Yeah mate I can hold it for ya.
There's an ATM down the road next to Maccas. Just give me twenty now and I'll put the stove back in the box for ya. Oh, and go get yourself a trolley when you come back yeah? I don't want you to bust your back carrying this thing mate.

Takes money and puts it into his bum bag.

Okay mate see ya then.

Waits for Customer 4 to leave. Meanwhile, Customer 2 is walking in the vicinity.

Fuck I love Aussies bro. He just paid for our lunch. We'll fix him up with the other stove in the box up the back when he shows up again. Help me hide this one under the—oh look! It's the Arab guy!
HEY! Hey brother! Come here, nah nah nah, come,
Come!
Look I can do the stove for seventy. It's the last one.
Brother I said I can't. I don't even get it for that much.
Okay, okay, look, sixty-five.
That's only five more than you asked!
Brother come on, I've come down twenty.

Pause.

Nah, go. Go.
I told you I can't brother. Just go.

Agitated, Abe waits for Customer 2 to leave.

Fucken dumb Arab—what a Jahaj. We're selling to peasants bro. Hey, come help me put this thing under the table.

Abe grabs the stove, turns 180 degrees and carries the stove to the back of the stall to place it under the collapsible table.

Yeah, just under here. Hey what do you want for lunch? I'm hungry. Do you wanna go get something down the road? I really feel like a Big Mac bro, just go get us something in twenty minutes—Oh fuck!

Abe turns around and pretends to casually walk up to the front of the stall where two policemen are waiting.

G'day, how you going gents?
Certainly is, I run the place, can I interest you with some steel capped boots officer?
No officer, no funny business here.
Those? Oh those are just leather gloves. Put on a pair, they go with your jacket.

Weapons?
Oh no way officer. No, no, they're just gloves! Come on, you can't hurt someone with those—it's just for fashion—for homosexuals and stuff you know?
No no, I mean, I'm not saying I think you're... I—that's not what I meant, sir.

Pause.

It's Abe.
Yes, Abe.

Pause.

I *am* being honest! That's my name! Look I'll show you my library card.

Abe waits impatiently as the policeman reads the card.

Yeah the first name is Aboud on there, that's what my friend's call me but Abe's my official name.
I swear officer, it's Abe Aboud Hamdam officially. Please!
Listen, I went to school in Erskineville and used Abe there, but when I moved to Lakemba the kids made fun of me so now I use Aboud.
But it's Abe on my birth certificate! I swear on my mother's grave!
Please, please, you don't have to confiscate the gloves, come on officer I wasn't trying to beat around the bush!
You can't be serious! They're just for people into their leather, I swear to god!
Oh god. Am I gonna be charged for selling these sir?
Oh god. No, no sir he doesn't.

Glances at the audience.

He just works here, he doesn't need to come up with us. Please, He's done nothing wrong—and I need someone to look after the stall while I'm gone.

Distressed, Abe picks up the box of studded gloves and walks up to the audience.

Oh fuck me bro. Look, they're gonna make me take the gloves up to the stall manager with them. Just look after the stall and if my dad calls, tell him I went to Hungry Jacks yeah? Bro I'm so fucked. My dad's gonna find out about this for sure. Oh god. Just—just take care of the stall alright?

Distraught, Abe walks off stage with the box.

UNTOUCHABLE

TANIA CAÑAS

(Silence. Character enters into silence from back of stage and takes in the surroundings.)

Airport. Two queues. I'm told to pick one.

Pardon?
No, I'm not from the Philippines, no not Cambodia, no I haven't been back to Thailand. I've never even been to Thailand.
Well, you know, I have a lot of Asian friends, I like noodles, I can use chopsticks, I'm a big fan of ramen so yeh, okay. I'll tell you I'm Asian.
You know,
Asian… by association.

El Salvador. A place I had to explain, a place that drew confused faces and a barrage of questions.
Central America. No, not literally the centre of the United States of America.
No, what you're pointing at right now is Africa.

(draws map)

Okay so here is North America and this is South America. There is a piece of land that connects them both.
No it's not just Mexico.
No, not Peru, you've gone too far.
But then again even the SBS world news weather report overlooks it, so what can I expect?
El Salvador. Fatty foods, failed revolutions, 80's time warp of bad hair and clothes as well as the infamous La Mara Salvatruha gangs. You know, the facial tattoos with the tear drop down one eye and the baggy clothes.
El Salvador barely makes it on Australian news, so when there was an article in the *mX* paper recently I felt a sense of pride.
It was an article in celebration of the first day in thirty years that someone had not been killed by gang violence. Finally some good news.

Airport. Two queues. I'm told to pick one.

I'm heading back for the first time in 23 years and sitting on a plane next to a man with a pudgy nose. He asks me about my passport.
'Oh, It's Australian.'
Australia. A place I didn't have to explain but a title I always had to fight for, and I've lived there most of my life!
(*draws breath*) The plane drops quickly.
Turbulence. I should have spent the extra two hundred for that TACA flight.
Pudgy nose looks at me
'An Australian passport? In El Salvador, that makes you untouchable.'

(*Looking down at passport she decides to put it away.*)

We land amidst the thick, lush grass and coconut trees. There is no city in sight, a contrast to LA, JFK and Melbourne airports. There is one very small, very underwhelming sign in blue and white that looks like it was taken straight out of Word Art. 'El Salvador'.
I look to the right from my aircraft window. There's a man wearing a cowboy hat calmly strolling through the grass with a machete in one hand and a half eaten apple in the other.
'The local lawn mower', explains pudgy nose.
All this is different to the grainy black and white photos, British voice over documentaries and rare tales told on a whim by relatives.
What I'm beginning to see in front of me is alive. It's moving. It's constantly changing.

Airport. Two queues. I'm told to pick one.

I step off the plane to be greeted by the airhostess who takes one look at my Australian passport and says
'Bienvenida Senorita Cañas'.
She pronounces my name right, that never happens in Australia.
Cañas, not *can-ass.*
I have to fill out a tourist card. I scan for a table but can't find one so I head to the nearest wall and fish for a pen.

I suddenly feel a large presence hanging over me.
Laced up leather boots that reach half way up his calf. Baton on one hip, pistol on the other. A cap, perfectly positions on his head.
Oh god, he thinks I'm writing on the wall.
—I'm not graffittiing! I'm sorry, I just—I was trying to find a table. And you know I—
'Can I see your passport?'
Stern. Unmoving. I can't read his face. It's giving nothing away.
'Are you by any chance Elena Cañas?'
I umm, i...
Three thoughts flash through my mind: ASIO has put my name on a no fly list. My passport is fake, someone has planted drugs in my bag.

(*lets out a sigh of relief.*)

Turns out he's been sent by my uncle to look out for me. He was told to look out for an Asian. Not an Asian Asian. A dark Asian. I guess he got it right cause he found me.

Airport. Two queues. I'm told to pick one.

The customs officer points to the alien queue. (*gestures to the right*) The Australian queue.
There are three guys with large surf boards under their arms and an elderly couple. No one comes to El Salvador unless you're a surfer or visiting family.
He then points to the queue for Salvadorians (*gestures to the left*) a line four times as long and four times as slow moving.
I look at the people in that line.
They are dark, short, have thick black hair and barely any necks—just like me.
I feel the sweat trickle down my back.

Airport. Two queues. I'm told to pick one.

(*She takes a step. Blackout.*)

BIRDCAGE

CHRISTOPHER HARLEY

LEWIS
(*ticked off*)
Say something, Dan.

Beat.

It was just a birdcage!
A fucking birdcage!
What are they, like, twenty dollars? Maybe forty at the most?

Beat.

You're still pissed off … aren't you.
You're still pissed off at me …

… aren't you.

Yeah, you're pissed.

Well, so am I.
I missed soccer and it was my last match of the year. Not the final, but we were playing for who comes seventh.

And you said you were gonna try and come for a bit before your date-thing and I know that you always say you'll come but then never do, whatever, but I thought that you might this time since, well, you know.

LEWIS starts rubbing one of his eyes.

Fuckin' dust. I hate dust.
Does Mum even vacuum anymore?
Ever?

LEWIS stops rubbing his eye; he looks up.

You were gonna come though, right?

You were, yeah?

Beat.

Fuckin' cops.
You should've seen how they handled me;
how they talked to me, asked me questions;
like I was some delinquent or some shit;
like I was trespassing.
I wasn't trespassing.
Okay, technically I was trespassing,
technically,
but if you think about it, I wasn't;
not really;
not heaps.

LEWIS rubs his eye again for a short moment.

Oh, and when it seemed like their fucking questions were about
to stop, I accidentally let it slip that I'm there, like,
heaps. And I don't even know why I said that, it's not even
true; I'm there like, five times a week maybe, like before
soccer or on the way home from school but then they start
asking another bunch of questions like 'Why do you sit
outside her house?' as if I'm some kind of stalker, which I'm
not, or like 'Have you ever wanted to harm her?' as if I was gonna
run over and punch her in the face or touch one of
her giant tits or something and so I say 'no' and they frown at
me and ask me the same question again as if that's gonna
make me say 'yes' so I say 'fuck off' and, well, that only
made things worse for while …
but she's, like, eighty-five and fat;
the last thing I want to do is touch one of her tits.

Fuckin' cops.

Fuckin' bitch. Fuckin' dumb bitch.
And I had to say it to her because no one else bothered to.
The neighbours must of heard her because she was so
fucking loud but they didn't say anything so I had to.

And no, I probably shouldn't have yelled,

I probably shouldn't have screamed right into her fat-face,
but if I didn't scream at her, who was going to?

And I've been patient.
I've been real patient.
For weeks.
Probably months.
I've just stood and watched.
Stood, watched and said nothing.
Sat and watched sometimes but whatever:
I still said nothing.
But sometimes you can't hold it in anymore.
Sometimes you just have to scream at someone's face.
Like, right in it.
So I did.
I screamed.
I screamed at an old woman and I still don't think I did
anything wrong.

Beat.

It's still the same, you know. I mean: it looks the same.
I haven't been that close since— … but it's still the same.
The grey, wooden verandah with all those rusty nails and
splinters and shit.
Those two chairs that we use to jump off and try and touch
the roof.
That bush—near the steps? the concrete ones?—that bush
with all those sugar-flower-things that we use to squeeze
and suck.
But not the grass: the grass is yellow.
She doesn't fuckin' take care of the grass.

Dad wouldn't have let that happen; dad *didn't* let that happen.
He was always watering the grass,
and if he couldn't do it he made one of us do it.
It was always green.
I don't remember it being any other colour.
But now an old bitch lives there and she let it go fucking
yellow.
Beat.

What time's your flight?
It's two in the morning so I figure it must be soon.

Beat.

Dan?

Beat.

Fine. Fucking fine.

Beat.

I've been doing it for years, you know.
Since, like—
And I don't do anything except sit in the gutter on the other
side of the road and try and throw gravel into the letterbox;
which is pretty much impossible to do but I still try 'cause I
figure if I get one in, then, I dunno, I won't need to go back
there anymore.
But since she moved in, I can't even throw rocks 'cause
she's always out the front doing, well, I don't know 'cause
she's not watering the fucking grass.

Beat.

Remember that night when Dad, like a week or something
before he left, Dad got home from the pub at, what, three or
four in the morning, drunk as hell, and decided he needed to
water the front yard?
And we found him in the morning when we were leaving for
school; passed out on the grass in a giant pool of water,
the hose still running.
He didn't say anything, remember?
He just got up and went inside.

Beat.

Anyway, the other day, like, two months ago maybe, I rode
there to sit in the gutter and whatever, and I get off my bike
and in the middle of our front yard there's this birdcage.
One of those big, fuck-off white ones.

Probably one of the forty dollar ones.
But it's empty.
And the door, the little door on the side: it's open.
And she's standing somewhere else, yelling:
'Paco! Paco! Paco!'
And it goes on for ages. I mean: *ages*.
She's running around the yard getting louder and louder with each yell.
She's looking behind bushes and under rocks, in the letterbox, yelling and yelling.
She shouts to the sky as if god is holding it hostage but the only response is a gust of wind as if he's all like, 'Fuck off, you old bitch. I don't have your bird'.
And I felt sorry for her at first. I did. But then she just got fucking irritating so I rode back home with fucking 'Paco-Paco-Paco' going round in my head.

I didn't sleep much that night.

But I go back the next day, right?
I go back in the arvo and the cage is still out there, still no bird, and she's in the same dress, yelling:
'Paco! Paco! Paco! Paco! Paco!'
And then I go back the next day and the next day and a couple days after that.
And I don't think she's in the same dress still.
I mean, I'm sure she's gone inside at some point.
She would of had to of, right?
But she's always out there, always screaming:
'Paco! Paco! Paco!'
Always looking under rocks and behind bushes and yelling at the sky and today … today I couldn't handle it.

LEWIS rubs his eye for a second.

I mean, I just couldn't.
I'm sitting out on the gutter watching her fucking show and she runs up on the verandah and lifts up one of the chairs to look under it.
One of our chairs. The chairs we use to jump off.
'Paco! Paco! Paco! Paco!' 'Fuck off!'

So I run. I run towards her.
I just couldn't—
I run towards her.
Not her: the cage.
The fucking birdcage.
I jump the fence and for fucking once she stops yelling and
I'm in the yard;
I'm standing in our yard for the first time since—and she
looks at me.
Finally she's shut the fuck up and she's looking at me.
And I throw the cage.
I throw it.
Hard.
At the ground.
I pick it up and throw it at the ground and it breaks into about
five pieces right at my feet.
             (*shouting*)
It's not coming back!!
The fucking bird is not fucking coming back so just fucking
shut the fuck up, okay?!
Just shut up, you fat fuck!
Things don't come back from here!
They go and they don't come back!
People go and they don't come back!
They walk out that door with a suitcase
and they don't come back!!
First Dad!
Then the fucking bird!
And now—

Beat.

Now you, Dan!!
You!!
Fucking *you*!
You're gonna catch a plan and then you're—

Beat.

             (*softer*)
You won't come back, Daniel.

42

Beat.

And I'm sorry. I'm sorry I fucked up your night. I'm sorry I made you late for your date and I'm sorry that I called *you* to pick me up and not Mum. I know you're pissed off but fucking hell, I called you because you're leaving tonight and I was trying to spend whatever three minutes I could get with you before you fly away for good.

It's 2am in the morning and I just want you to talk to me.
Say something, Dan.
Say something!
Fucking—fucking say goodbye to me.

Beat.

Please.

Pause.

LEWIS starts rubbing his eye.

There's something in my eye.

Beat.

Fuckin' dust.

THIS FERAL LIFE

JULIA-ROSE LEWIS

Mia, a 17-year-old girl wearing a school uniform stands in a graveyard during the day, she begins to talk whilst removing her school socks and shoes.

Always wag down here, no-one looks in the graveyard. The sun shines brighter, *best* spot for sunbaking. Come when shit gets lame at school. She kept saying 'Nurse? Psychologist?, Teacher'—as if!… annoying. Want it to be easier. Want to drink more, dance more, sleep more. 'Photography is not a stable career' that bitch told me. She said, 'what about journalism instead?' I said, I don't give a shit about the news. She said, 'don't swear Mia.' I said, rack off! She said, 'Mia? Is this about your dad?, It's okay to feel angry.' Her face. She had *that* look on her face. Don't look at me with that face! I stood up, pushed a chair over and left. Had to get out. Didn't actually *mean* to push the chair over, but didn't bother to pick it up.

I'm not planning on working weekend shifts at Hungry Jack's for the rest of eternity like some of those moles will. Never get out. I'm not gonna make-manager buy a fucking restaurant, become a fat lard who's been flipping patties for 40 years and never seen the world. Na, I'll get out. I work drive through, that's a big deal you know. Only the chicks who take smoke breaks with Ted our boss get asked to do drive through. So I started. Smoking I mean. It worked. Stole the durries from dad, Winny Reds, 16mils, fuck me. Nearly died. Watched the way you held the cigarette in your mouth. Inhale, say something, hold it in. Exhale. I. Was. A. Natural.

Welcome to Hungry Jack's, place your order/ Listen Customer at the window/ $14.95 please/ P plates at the speaker talking. Listen to the order. Fuck. Listen. Concentrate/

'Ah can we have like, two Bacon Deluxes, wiv cheese, yeah wiv cheese. Oh wait hold on… babe you want cheese? Babe cheese!? Oh no wait only one wiv cheese.'/

Concentrate, take the order. Customer at the window getting impatient. Talk to them Mia/ Cash or Credit?/ P plates in my ear again/

'and um can we get… soft serve in the cokes, like a coke float, ya know?'

(*Pause*)

'Does that cost extra?'/

Yes. Fuck. It costs extra! We don't give ice-cream away dipshit.

It's full stressful. Only messed up a few times. Think I'm pretty good. Dad was stoked when I got drive through. Went out for steak to celebrate. No big deal, but he was full proud. Still, I'm not dumb enough to think I can't do better, one day. I'm gonna be something awesome, I'll be great. I'll be famous probably. Gonna buy a camera. Photograph people that have a good story in their wrinkles. Sell them, make a book. Art galleries you know… (*She throws her hands in the air*)… success.

(*Beat*)

I'm not a Goth, I don't come here at night. I'm not like that.

(*She pauses realising that the topic is grim*)

I'm actually okay. I'm not messed.

This shit just happens. I'm sick of that face. That 'Oh, so sorry for your shitty life' face. Hate that face. Want to smash that face when I see it. The chicks at school and that counsellor have it, wear it all day long looking at me. Moles. Just look at me! Just look at me normal! Just talk to me normal! I'm not a fuck up! Stop waiting for me to break. Stop waiting for me to break up into little pieces and blow away. I've got this one. I'm actually okay.

I think pretty loud thoughts but they all call me quiet. At school the girls whisper about me being quiet. Not talking. I'm actually not though.

(*She traces her fingers along an engraving on a headstone.*)

'To Love well is to place a hand on another's chest and know that the heart only beats when locked in a cage of bone'

Gonna get a tattoo of that just here

(*She lifts up her shirt and runs her fingers along her rib cage.*)

They don't know what's coming to them those girls. I think about it, not in a sick way, but I think about all the fucked up shit that's gonna happen in their lives. I already know, but they have no idea what's coming to them. They can't see it coming. I can though. See their parents dying, heart attacks, strokes, their kids dying, teenagers drunk in cars dying, overdoses, their dogs dead, hit and run, car crashes, cancer, babies born munted, husbands cheating, I feel like I can see it all. It's why I don't hate them. I know what's coming. It's totally unavoidable though, all that shit. I actually feel pretty wrecked for them.

All these graves, all these people. All these lives, these broken lives. These feral lives. Hundreds and hundreds of them.

From that hill over there you can see my school. It was actually used as a hospital during the war. Men jumped over those balconies. To die. Too fucked up to keep living. They just gave up. Some of those men are buried in this place. (*She points nearby*) Over there, a whole family buried in that grave over there. A man and a women, eight kids. That man died when he was young, like really young, so fucked, and all eight of their kids, dead before 20, but that women, that mum, she lived until she was 99. She buried her whole family. *All* of them. Carved above her name?… 'duty courageously served'.

(*Mia checks her phone.*)

I bet she wished she was dead, lots of times. She could have killed herself. People would, I'm sure other people would.

The people in these holes… their bodies would just be earth. Just rock and dust and bone and just ground, all mixed in. Did you know when your body is embalmed, like the people in those big above ground graves over there, you last for ages apparently. You last forever, but if they open it up, the coffin, if they have to open it up for whatever reason, the second the air hits you, the oxygen, the particles or whatever you were just turn to dust. Just like that... BAM! Dust.

That stupid counsellor bitch at school would have something to say about me coming here if she knew she'd say that I was 'grieving', 'not coping'. I'm sure she would have some bullshit to share (*Mia mimics the counsellor*) 'His light will always shine brightly in your soul Mia.' What a load of wank. He's dead lady. He's not embalmed, he's actually in this ground, been here for 3 months. Rotting. He has. No light. He didn't even have one when he was alive dumbass.

He's just dead

(*Mia throws a rock into the distance, and another, and another. She turns away from the audience and lights a cigarette.*)

I've got a double drive through shift this weekend. I'll get a pay rise when I graduate. Over 18's get a pay rise. Awesome. Save to buy a camera. A good one. Gonna buy a plane ticket, get my tattoo, yeah, double shifts are rad.

(*Mia sits down she pulls her school skirt up slightly to reveal more of her thighs and leans back as if basking in the sun.*)

It's always so bright in here. *Best* spot for sunbaking.

THE MANGROVES

TOM MESKER

ALISON:

> 'Twas brillig, and the slithy toves
> Did gyre and gimble in the wabe:
> All mimsy were the borogoves,
> And the mome raths outgrabe.

Miss sits there reciting to the class like she's about to climax. Each word drawn out like a moan. Any wetter and she'll slide off her seat.

Alison Brennan, did you just put your gum under the desk?
Great. And no bitch I put it up my ass.
You can stay back and clean that off.

The bathrooms have a cloud of smoke hanging above them. I wash my hands after getting hard, crusty gum off that desk and examine the ink all up these sickeningly pastel walls. Kelly Grodden's a mank ass cunt. This was never at my old school. Millie Marks is a slut. I trace 'slut' with my wet finger.

'snot true.
My new bestie. All uffish 'n shit. Stubbing her cig out.
Jess does suck mank dick but.
I laugh.
Come to the Mangas when ya done finger painting 'tard.
She flicks her hair and I see her ass as she twirls and walks out. I look in the mirror and through Millie's lingering cig haze I see my Mum.

I know its tough Al, but make the most of this new school.
Whatever. If you weren't such a dumb docile ho Dad wouldn't have left you and I wouldn't be here. What have you made the most of lately? She fades.

I'd already heard about the Mangas. The cool kids hang there. Smoke 'n shit. Climb through and wag class. Invite only. I roll the top of my skirt up under my blouse so the hem rises to just under my vag. Flick my hair and twirl out.

I strut my shit across the oval and see Millie with a bunch of guys and some other girl that's way hotter than Millie, they are all looking at her, so she's the leader. Sarah Donovan.

Hey new girl. Mills told me you're a bit badass hey? Where you from?
Vaucluse.
She looks vague.
Over the Bridge.
Ohk.
Frabjous.

We weave our way into the mangroves. I'm not gonna lie. I fucking hate being dirty and I hate smells, like smelly smells. I'm covered in stinky mud all over my white socks and new shoes. We used to leave school and go to a café. Café Prego. The boys from Scots would walk us up to the oval where we'd sit on the bench and watch them being douches. These plebs climb ahead of me further into the mangroves, twisting and turning, flicking mud on each other while crabs scurry and dive into their holes. I'm behind Dean Hughes who's this hot babe, he's a surfer. Real tanned and blonde and I can see his wettie tan across his neck. He helps me through this tricky part and into the clearing. The sun filters through the branches and you can see the river that links up to the beaches through the trees. The sun dancing and bouncing off the wet. It would be really beautiful apart from the smell, the sludge, the abandoned bongs, coke cans, food wrappers, used doms and alc bottles spattered about. Dean hands me the drinkbottlehosealfoil bong, I flick my hair to one side and pull back on the cone, show these Beaches drongos what I'm made of, make the most of it. Before we go I tell Dean to add me on Facebook and wink. I don't usually wink. It's weird and kind of slutty. YOLO.

At home I have six new friend requests and Dean talks to me on chat.
How u?
Mum calls me down for dinner. Worst timing.

Brb.

I eat in our shitty townhouse laminate and lino kitchen, we used to have Caesar Stone and you couldn't see the fridge because it was hidden behind a door. I look at this sad woman. What happened to her? No strength. I push the dinner around on my plate. Can't hold onto Dad and can't cook a meal. She talks about how She's got three job interviews lined up and how we can redecorate the shitty townhouse. Callooh. Callay.

Dean's gone offline. No messages from my old friends. No likes. I write on their walls.

New school is so fucking lame. Such povvo losers! Catch-ups soons? xxx, A.

Bell. Class. Bell. Recess. Smoke in the dunnies. Call Kelly Grodden a slut. Bell. Mangas. Bell. Miss creaming her pants. Bell. Mangas. Home. Bell. Dean meets me at the gate. Jaberwock. Bell. Txt. Mangas. Bell. Mills passes notes. Bell. Home. Shitty townhouse.

I screw up the note from Mum and put the lasagna in the bin.

Be safe, text me when you get to Millies. I'm home at 10. Call if you want. Love you. xxx.

Mills arrives we steal vodka out of the pantry, dance in my room, take selfies, do each others make up. She says the dumbest shit. Wants to be a hairdresser.

Dean likes you, Al. Told me. Will you mack him tonight? Make sure Sarah don't see you but, hey. She totally broke up with him ages ago but fully likes him still. No-one messes with Sar.

Sure.

Mills gets out the pills I told her to get. I dump one. So does she. She squeals. I LOL.

The music is fucking blaring, hurts my ears. It's all gangsta shit but we're right near the beach. I don't get it. There's heaps of people. Open house. At least a 100. Apparently dumbslut Kelly posted it on facebook, didn't make it private. The house is big. Looks over Pittwater right across the dog park, Mangas to the right and the grotsky school beyond that. Mills grabs my hand and we weave our way through the crowd. Twisting, turning, we get to a clearing. Deans there.

Hey.

Hey.
Sars behind him.
He gives me his drink. I sip, pull him in close and we kiss. Its all bourbon and cokey. He runs his hands down my back over my ass and up the back of my skirt. I press my hips in hard to his groin and catch a look at Sar. Frumious.

I grab Dean and we weave through limbs, the beat pulses, the high kicks in, I'm so fucking mimsied, no likes, no messages, I float and duck and weave, so high, brillig, I push past the dipshits the public school proles, the branches grab and slap, snicker-snack twigs snap, the Scots boys toss the ball on the oval and the café Prego coffee mud flicks up as we galumph through and through this tulgey wood and my jaw jabberwocks from side to side.
Come to my arms, my beamish boy!
The sludge is cold, Caesar Stone cold.
We rest against a TumTum tree in the middle of the wabe.
His claws they catch and grabe my tits.
Slithy, slithy, slithy.
The wide tree lined streets.
His vorpal sword in my snatch, my bandersnatch.
One, Two! One, Two!
Through and through.
I'm coming home from the café, Dad's Beamer's in the drive and Mum's making dinner.
He chortles in his joy.
He leaves me dead and with my head he goes galumphing back.

I'm covered in slop. I float down from mingling with the branches above. Lying in my silly fucking wonderland. Wetness licks my toes. It tickles but it's lapping at my ankles now. The tide. No one told me about the tide. A crab patters down my arm, across my hand and over my phone. It lights up. Txt. Mum. Al? xxx.

I see you now Mum. The roots and branches make up your limbs. And I see you clear against the moon. You stand and sway and just look at me. Like I've looked at you. Both of us looking, making the most of it.

I'm okay. Love you. xxx, A.

THESE THINGS HAPPEN

JOEL PERLGUT

Lights up on sliding doors and a railing. QUINN *a young man in full clown gear, enters. From behind the doors we hear children laughing, singing 'Happy Birthday', the sound extinguished when the doors close.*

QUINN:

Spoilt shits. Jumping on my shoes, pulling my hair. Dad's a corporate fraud and mum's all hot flushes and have-a-slice-of-cake. Soon as you wear a costume you're a piece of meat.

Aren't you a bit young to be a clown? A boy like you, so handsome, could be anything. She writes her number on the back and sticks the cheque down my pants. Tell me a joke, make me laugh, eat me out.

Quinn walks up to the railing.

Will you look at that? It's the kind of sheer drop only money can buy. Only way to make a view like that better is a cigarette. It's tempting but I quit. For the kids. Some days I don't care, I figure why not? I'll hit Elizabeth Street so hard my face'll slide off. A beautiful death mask, big black tears and big red smile. It is tempting.

I wasn't always a clown. I used to be quite funny. I used to be a pretty relaxed guy. At high school my apathy was legend. Exams came and went and I barely notice. Talk of a career. Travel or uni or working at Maccas until you self immolate in the deep fryer. It's all just noise. Schoolies and ATAR and suddenly everyone's smoking joints instead of bongs.

That's when it happened. Not like growing pubes, a slow but sure ascent to manhood, I just woke up with them one day.

Quinn flaps around his oversized shoes.

Size 19. It's not even a real size. Inconvenient? Yes, undeniably. Had to get shoes ordered from Norway. Custom made. Two hundred dollars plus shipping. They're too small, wear out in a week. No point in causing a fuss. I had a little growth spurt. These things happen.

Next it was the hair. I wake up in a sea of green fuzz. It's a grooming nightmare, feels like plastic, can't get a brush through. But I'm not that precious. I never cared much for the old stuff anyway, always forgetting to get it cut, never knew what shampoo to buy. Don't even have to wash it, doesn't get oily or smell.

I've always had a rule about body modification. No piercings, no tats, no reason, just not for me. So the make up came as a shock. I'll admit, my cool was shaken. My eyes sting from the soap, my fingers are raw. Nothing. It's stuck. What's the point? People notice, stare, my parents, friends. They worry about me, about my future. Where are you going with this? You trying to be funny or something?

I say I'm a clown. I say I like to make people laugh. What else can I do?

I pick it up quickly, YouTube tutorials, how-to ride a unicycle, flowers out of a hat, I'm a natural. Pick out a suit, polka dots or stripes? I take both. They're comfy. I don't take them off, what's the point?

I start with a friend's sister's party. Word gets around. Cut price clown, too young to be a pedo, the kids love him. Advertise on notice boards, Gumtree, the Herald. I trade in my sedan for a mini with a novelty horn. People eat that shit up. Soon it's yuppie Christmas parties, pro bono at the hospital on weekends. Good money too. Clowning is a boom industry. You'd be surprised, people are sad, they'll do anything not to think about it.

Quinn clutches the railing with both hands, leans over.

You know I think I will have that cigarette.

Quinn checks his pockets, pulls out a coloured handkerchief, attached to another and another, they keep on coming. He stops.

And there's a girl. Did I mention that? I mean there's always a girl. She'd been away for a while, six months. Picking apples in Finland, posing with Kafka in Prague, flamenco dancing in Seville. Needed to find herself, see the world.

My fault really, should have written in advance. Didn't think to mention it. I meet her at the arrivals gate, flowers, chocolate, a card: *Missed you this much* and a picture of a fisherman bragging about his trout. Maybe I will tell her I bought them at the servo on the way, she'll find it endearing. Me, the loveable slacker.

What a metamorphosis, she looks great, taller, tanned, confident. Takes a while for her to recognise me. She screams. Not like her, generally pretty relaxed, I'm flattered of course but then she doesn't stop. Security asks if everything is okay. EVERYTHING IS FINE, barely heard above the screech. WHAT WAS THAT? How was I meant to know?

Quinn opens a tiny pocket dictionary to a bookmarked page.

Claurophobia, noun, the abnormal or exaggerated fear of clowns.

She makes me get on a different train carriage. She won't let me walk her to the door. I call later and she cries. Then I cry. We decide to work it out.

She sees a shrink who gets her to juggle. She sees a hypnotherapist who swings a red nose in her face. She sees a DVD of *Patch Adams*. I tie my hair in a ponytail. I put on a balaclava. I turn up to her place in my dad's Toyota and a skinny tie.

She tells me the Thames is filthy and that she saw a dead body, her first. I tell her I own three miniature tricycles. I'm excited, getting first date *déjà vu*. She kisses me through the fabric, presses against me. My gloved hands squeeze her breasts.

Quinn honks twice on a bright red horn.

My water pistol flower goes off in her face. I'm so sorry, that's never happened before, I promise. Try to mop it off with a handkerchief but they just keep on coming and coming and besides it's stuck. It's stuck on her face and I can't do anything about it. She's petrified and I've never felt so terrible and I'm looking, hoping, that under the tears she'll break into a big red smile. She'll tell me everything is fine, she was just having a laugh.

I'm a clown. I know that now. I make people laugh. I make people scream. I make people throw up lasagna in the toilet for half an hour. I make them change phone numbers. I make them tell their friends to tell me it's not my fault, that sometimes [*pause*] these things happen.

Quinn goes back to the railing.

You didn't think I was gonna jump did you? The whole 'painting Elizabeth Street with my body' thing? That was just a joke. Bad taste I'll admit but I couldn't resist the cliché. Besides, I'm on the clock.

SILO

CHARLES PURCELL

Tyson, 18, disheveled and agitated, in a silo. He reaches up and runs a thumb across his bottom lip.

TYSON:

Nothing out here but dirt and flies.
Dirt and flies and sticks and shit.

Shit and empty cans.

And thoughts.
Loud thoughts.
Different thoughts to town thoughts;
Thoughts like boulders banging through the brain,
Banking up and 'bout to burst.

Rip the lid off a can,
Pour the beans in my mouth.
Sharp edge slices my lip—*fuck*—and as I pelt the can against the wall the clang crashes up the metal.

Look outside,
Lick the blood off my lip.
My tongue finds the tear,
The salty wet swell.

And I want you to taste it,

(Beat)

I want you to taste it.

Over against Mt Kaputar the chime clangs and dies.

Sun's rearing its head,
Dirt's glowing red.
And there you are:

(Beat)

We did it,
You and me.
We're the ones that got out.
You and me flying free down the Barwon.
Two outback hoodlums flying free out of Narrabri
And into the empty—

(Beat)

Look, I made us a calendar.
Y'see?
It's simple.
Just for the seasons.
It's to help us survive.
But it'll help us keep track of the days, too.
Keep track of how long it's been since *things* happened.
Big things.

Today it's a week since we made that plan.
A week today since we made that plan *together* and you bit my
lip and—

(Beat)

You must be close,
So I'll just sit here.
Sit right here on the silo steps and look out towards town.

Sun's getting higher,

And there you are:

That day.
Cumby Races,
Tongues dry with dust.
Smells like hay and horse shit.
Engines revving,
Utes spinning,
Farmers' kids everywhere spilling bourbon from cans.

And there you are on a bale on the back of a ute.
Smug as fuck,
Just one of them.
But as the horses roar past,
I turn and through the dust,

You're looking at me.

(*Beat*)

You're looking at me,
Smiling.

And I know in that moment
We're gunna get out.

You and me free.
You and me free flying out of that town and into the empty.

And it's just us from then.
Just our little secret.

But the secret weighs heavy and we can't fight free.

Not us.

Not there.

Not us, there.

And one night it hits us,
It hits us like a slap:
We'll just do it.
We'll leave.
We'll leave and start afresh.
No exams no phones no bullshit no school.
No one to answer to no one to hide from.
No parents no people.
We'll build our own house,
And we'll grow our own food.
Just us alone in the middle of nothing.
And we laugh and talk fast and it's probably a joke.

An absurd perfect forlorn downright stupid joke.
But we laugh harder and harder,
'Cause it could just be—

Just you and me:

Two outback hoodlums on the run.

(*Laughs*)

And,

I think we both *know*,
That it doesn't have to be a joke
That we could actually go,
We could go if we wanted.
And then—*bang*—it's real,
We're packing and it's real.
We'll slip out Friday night while the whole town's asleep,
And we'll meet at the silo just outta town.

(*Pause*)

Get to the silo as the sun's coming up.
Can see it across the cold scorched red,
Like a lonesome rocket: mammoth and still,
Base black from a fire like it once tried to take off.

No road no house no soul in sight.

Climb up the stairs.
Put down the swag.

And I wait.

Walk circles round the rocket and I wait.
Throw rocks and hear the clang and I wait.

All morning I wait,

kicking rocks
kicking shit
eating beans

banging sticks

and

the sun the fucking sun
it moves lower,
and lower.

And—

Night comes.

(*Beat*)

But you don't.

(*Pause. He reaches up and runs a finger across his lip.*)

It was our chance to get out,
Together.
We had that key to escape together and start again,
Start our own little cosmos,
Just you and me.
You and me free,
You and me free flying out of that town and into the empty.

But—
That dirt swallowed your feet and reset at your ankles
Just like it'll do to me if I ever go back.

So I gotta push on.
Push on down the Barwon.

(*He touches his lip.*)

Lip scabbed rough.
Blood crusted hard.
So tomorrow I go.

Without you.

PEACH

IZZY ROBERTS-ORR

*El is sitting on a park bench, outside the markets. She is holding
a peach in one hand, a bunch of grapes in the other. A bag of
oranges at her feet.*

*She slides the bunch of grapes over to the other side of the
bench and looks at them, accusing. She devours the peach.*

El sniffs the air.

Cinnamon. Fish. And piss.
I dunno how anyone could think it was a good idea to piss on
the back wall of the seafood hall. To add to the stink and the
brine.
Maybe it's the only place to lean against the wall and let it out.
Because it already smells unclean.
They work in white aprons and white boots, white so they can
see the smears of black-red fish guts and clean it off at the end
of the day.

El pulls a pouch of tobacco from her pocket.

White so they glow in the fluorescent doorway's smoko haze.
White so they look cleaner than the shit they trudge through
all day.
White so they get lost in the tiles and the ice of the screaming,
fishmongering hall.

El starts to empty the tobacco on the ground, slowly, methodically.

Left, towards cinnamon.
Kick a burning butt into the steaming piss-river mingling with
the salt scales of dead-eyed silver fish.
Head spin, still drunk, fresh bread
and my stomach turns over.

El rubs her nose.

Fingers smell like tobacco,

not sure if I like it.
But it's mine.
I wanna smoke.
I want your smokes, your champion ruby cigarettes,
scattered packets on our coffee table,
smell of damp and paper and your socks—
she stopped trying to clean your room.
I want to breathe in that smoke, breathe you in that smoke.

El stamps on the tobacco, grinding it into the wet ground.

Left again, here again,
sticky floor and sweat again.
32 per cent of residue in public spaces is semen.
Dim red and blue light—
why do bars always have red and blue lights?—
Nothing is happening. Nothing is actually happening.
Him. At the end of the bar.
Hair like James Dean—
buy me a drink?—
I hold it like a question mark
I skull it like air.
Swimming in bourbon,
nose burning, back of my throat.
Pins prick eyes.

Another drink.
Hands like shovels.
Fat and pale. Grimy.
I don't notice his eyes.
Hand in pocket—
buy me another?—
He is James Dean from Warnambool,
He is skinny jeans and blundstone boots and a leather jacket
and I wanna sink my teeth in him.—
wanna go outside?—
He looks at me like 'what for?'—
for a ciggie. Got some?—
got a whole pouch, you can bum one.—

Peach

I sink my teeth in.
Skin punctures and luscious, wet flesh peels into my mouth.
It's dripping. So sweet.
I can't contain the juice, so I lick my fingers instead.
Syrupy, down my throat, my tastebuds are fucking…
well, they're loving it—
They're fucking. Yeah. My tastebuds are fucking this peach and
loving it.
There's an orgy in my mouth.
I moan.
At least I think I moan.
Maybe the sound was in my head, I sort of hope
it was in my head.—
Y'know there's nine thousand bodies buried under those
markets— you're beautiful, he says.
So I grab him and I suck his face into mine and I bite his lip—
Ouch! Don't do that.—
Shovel hands rolling ruby cigarettes.
Put his hands on me, pull him in,
take him from himself—
what are yo–
drag him round the corner,
dark here, cold but him warm
no blue light, no disco,
boot kick water, faces like magnets,
attract, repel, repel, attract,
collide.

I am walking on air.

Clammy fingers on me,
I dig mine in—
huh.—
Pulse climbing my throat
His face, my neck, biting,
He's bruising me.
Bruise me. Bruise me, peach.
Back grating against a cold concrete wall—
grazed, just here, at the base.
We are in each other, everywhere,

my heart pouring out of me like sand,
me and him against this wet wall—

and I remember you cutting your toenails.

Cutting your toenails with big, strong hands.
Long fingers. Knuckles like marbles.
Ugly hands. Ungainly hands.
Knotted hands covered in freckles, chewed nails.
I remember you cutting your toenails in the sun,
Sun through your curls,
Long muscles, long bones hacking at your toes.—
Ohmygod, ew! What are they *doing*—
door open, music blare—
Slam.

Wet sky falls over us,
sour breath, rough face,
hands stick to leather, don't slide.
Scrape fingernails on denim,
find a gap in the seams, a pocket, a pouch
gripping his face I am slipping his smokes
into my jacket pocket.

Limp condom on the ground,
plastic bagging gagging fluid.
Swallow me, night—
Oi, Lovebird we're leaving—
Huh. Huh. Huh.
Dead dog stench in my pores
I am bursting into sun
I am free.
Huhhh.
Leg shaking,
mouth grasping
He is done.

I vomit.
Zip fly, flick hair—
[Him] Can I have your number?—

I smoke.
Bass dies, bar empties
drunks roll hips home.

I smoke.
Streetlight haze dissolves.

I smoke.
Delivery driver spits.

I smoke.

I smoke.
I smoke.

I smoke.

I

PRIVATE RESEARCH

RANDA SAYED

Marwer is in the hallway of Zoe's house…

Ahh Zoe, sorry, I just walked into your brother's room by accident, the bathroom is the door to my…?
Second to the left! That's right. Got it!
Yeah sure you can, I saved our draft under 'World War I Presentation.'
No, I have no password; just flip it open, it should come up.

Marwer enters. She runs to her computer and slams it shut.

Ah—
Did you—
But—
Ca—
I didn't—
I—
I forgot I—
I was just—just researching it for a—a Sports Science assignment—the assignment—it's an assignment—an assignment on Yoga! Yoga and how you… need to learn how to… yes, how to touch yourself—no! How—how you need to know your anatomy through exercising and doing… Yoga.

It's not funny. I'm hilarious am I? Who the hell are *you* to laugh at me? You don't give a shit cause you Aussie girls do it all the time, you—you—you have boyfriends and short denim shorts hiked up to your bums!

(*Beat*)

I'm sorry Zoe. I didn't mean that. It's just, it's okay for *you*, it's not for me.

No! Never! I don't do it. I just wanted to know more about it!

It's not normal for us, it's haram—against our religion.

Zoe, you can't tell anyone about this, no one, not even your friends—what difference does it make? Leila hangs out with you sometimes and she sits with the Leb group, the Maso girls and the smart Asian group they all hang out with you guys and some of them talk to my friends and if my friends *know* it could get to my parents. Yes it will! My cousins are on Facebook and I don't have privacy settings—I don't have them 'cause it just looks like I have something to hide—if my friends write something on my wall my cousins will see it and Janice, she knows my brother and my brother will go to my Dad—don't tell me to calm down!

If anyone hears about this…

It is a big deal. They won't see it like you do. They will call me a…

Huh?

They'll… call me a… Zoe, I know I don't know you well but I hope I can trust you. Can you promise me that you will not say a word about this to *anyone*? Please?

Really? Not even your mum?

Thank you. Thank you so much. You're a lifesaver.

(*Beat*)

I told you I was— okay. I was looking it up because of… Amanda. Last week we were in Exploring Early Childhood, learning about pregnancy and… the process of getting pregnant. We were doing an exercise and I opened the text-book. I saw a picture of… of… it was the first time I had seen a male private part. It looked like my old Pluto toy from the Mickey Mouse Club house. of the pictures showed Pluto's head inflated. The other, Pluto's head deflated.

This is so embarrassing. I have no idea why I am saying this to you. Yeah, keep this secret too, thanks.

So, Amanda saw me jump out of my seat a bit. She came over and slid into an empty chair next to me,

'Marwer! What's wrong?'
'Oh! Are you scared of that?'
'Have you never seen one before?'
'Oh, was that your first time!'
'That is so weird!'
'Oh! But you know what sssseex is—'

She looks at Zoe.

She kept asking things and raising her voice every time I said 'no'! She made sure everyone could hear her, pretending to be nice but (*Marwer leans in and whispers*) she was really being a bitch. Asma and Rima were looking at me from the corner of the room. What could they say? So yeah, I was just checking that stuff online because I just want to know my shit more.

No way, not in class. I looked it up last period in the library, top level, before we met up.

(*Beat*)

Do you do it? No! No. I mean… do you research it…masturbat— that was a stupid question.

(*Beat*)

Do you like your room? It's more than okay, its awesome! I love the blue and orange colour scheme! Very Mexican, like, out of a Home and Living magazine and this poster, I can't stop looking at it. She is a Spanish dancer, isn't she? That's right, a Flamenco dancer. She is so… her face… it's like she knows, she knows she is being looked at but she is not defensive or trying to be anything, she's just… open and aware.

(*Beat*)

These windows they're called 'Bay windows', aren't they? I bet you lay down on this cushiony thing here and read and lookout all day. Can I open the window?

Marwer opens the window and looks out.

Nice. Nah, it's awesome! At least you can see the horizon and the rooftops. At my home, all you can see is the opposite veranda and the small Asian lady that lives there. All she does is hang her daughter's washing up… (*Marwer leans in and whispers*)… and she smokes cigarettes. I have seen her do it almost every night. At around twelve she opens her sliding door really quietly and slinks out. You hear a metal click. Then all you see is the bright orange end of her cigarette swirling around.

(*Beat*)

I think I used to do it. When I was little, I would scratch it. Maybe, I was scratching it because it felt… maybe I was masturbat—I don't know.

I showed my mum once 'cause it was hurting me. She told me that if I touched it, I could ruin it and—

A loud beep of a horn.

My Dad! Shit! What time is it? It's 6:30?

She grabs all her stuff.

Maybe, maybe Thursday, I'll ask my dad.

She stops and looks at Zoe.

See you around school tomorrow?

SUNRISE SET

KRYSTAL SWEEDMAN

A bedroom.
A window. It is dark outside. Early hours of the morning.
The final call.
An old lady lies in bed; she may be slightly propped up.
She may not be.
The room is furnished as old ladies like it.
Lace doilies supporting satin lined jewellery boxes and silver handled brushes. Potpourri, and paraphernalia gathered from adventures abroad.
Sarah Betts rushes in, laptop in hand.
She sees her gran, momentarily shocked by how bad she looks, she forces a smile and kisses her on the cheek.

I'm here, I'm here
It's okay
Look what I've got
Every visit you make me promise and
Well
I know it's been a while
But
I've made it
Can I sit?
I'll sit

(*She sits on the potty chair, unaware of its purpose.*)

It shouldn't take long
It's only three minutes
Do we have three minutes?
Sorry
Stupid question
Here, here it is (*She opens her laptop*)

What's the password?
Shit— sorry.
Password… password…

Dalphene, Norm, hmm, Cleo— not the cat,

Mutley, wrong dog, what was the last dog she had…

Sorry sorry sorry
It's coming
You could tell me
Okay
Um,
Password

(*Beat*)

Of course
Why did you change the password to password?
Anyway

Here
(*She types in the address*)
It's on YouTube
Not quite TV
But it's today's TV
Only interactive and
It doesn't matter
Listen

(*Beat*)

The sound of a crowd is heard and a band trying out a few notes.
It stops.

No no no nononnononononoNO!
Come on.

(*She takes a breath—calmer.*)

Sorry gran it just needs to buffer,
Won't be long.
Hold on hey.
(*She squeezes her hand*)

Had it for a month

Kept

Meaning to bring it
But
sorry
stupid
Didn't expect you to
Before we

Remember the Rodeo Grounds?
That's where it is

(*Beat*)

Here we go

We hear the same sounds as before, but now we get a few seconds of guitaring and drums.

It stops.

For the love of god!
Sorry Gran
I love god. I do
I just wish he'd make our Internet work faster

(*Hands and face to the sky aka god*)
Why. Can't. You. Control. The. Things. That. Really. Matter?

If we get a few frames in you'll be able to see the crowd. It's full.
The whole arena.

You would love the outfits this year.
Sparkles and country music—who'd have thought it?
Nice wholesome girls getting round in skinny jeans and sparkly shirts.
It's kinda like they've replaced tassels.
Mind you, there are still plenty of old cowboys, tassels wavin with the breeze.

I leave the country singing to the cowgirls

And beg my way into the *Anything But* section.

Supposed to be for 18+

And I'm only a few months a way
but you know… rules

I mention your name Gran
They're so awestruck they let me enter
And suggest we do a duet

Would you like that?

I'll even sing that country song
Despite what I said

(*Beat*)

It should work now…

She tries for the third time. We hear the crowd, the introduction of the song and just as the first note is about to be sung… the Internet fails again.

Faaark—arty gumdrops.

Um.

Well
There's me anyway

I'm wearing the shirt you gave me—see?

We're playing like our hearts depend on it
You can't see him, but our cameraman; Trent, is standing on the dirt below the stage
He's brilliant
He's my age, but he has a huge following on YouTube. He makes really sweet short films.
If we can get through this one, I'll show you some of his others.
You'd like them.

And before you say 'ooh, is that a little tenderness in your voice Betsy?'

I'll say yes, yes it is. Whether he has tenderness for me, I'm not sure.

He is brilliant though; we had to stitch two pieces of film together.
Right at my favourite spot in the song.
You can barely notice it on this.

After the first chorus
A thunderstorm blows in and dumps itself all over the arena.
No one is ready for it; the whole crowd gets soaked.

And even though everyone runs for shelter—they're just making it worse for themselves.

We stop; 'cause the wind is using the rain as bullets and us as targets
and well

As much as I love the smell of red dirt rising in the air, I am really disappointed.
I want this so badly for you Gran.

(Beat)

Fifty percent buffered.

What you don't see on this,
Is Sheryl

Climbing up on stage
Taking hold of the microphone like it's a blind man's hammer
And clearing her throat. Several times.

She asks everyone to come back and take a seat

Says that this is a very important set
For a very important person.
You may know her as the great Casey May

But to this young lady, she's just Nan
And she's performing here tonight to fulfil her gran's final wish.

They came back in droves. Covered in mud and soaked to the bone.
Respectful.
I guess that's one good thing about Mareeba.
It's so hot
They'll dry by the end of the song anyway.

And so we play again

and if you look at the second half of the song Gran you'll notice that my eyes are playing up
They're doing that thing they do
When they can't control themselves
And they well up
And they blur my vision

And as the audience get their phones out and start waving them to the music,
They sing along, even though they're hearing the words for the first time
All I feel is warmth and all I can think of is all those times you told me I could sing, and all those times you promised you wouldn't die until you saw me on TV.

You promised. You have to keep your promise
You have to hold on until it buffers
It may not be country but it's

me

Hold on
Please?

(*Beat*)

Gran's life support machine starts to beep.

It's not gunna—

Sarah leans in and sings softly to her grandma. The sun rises behind the window.

With the passing of the wind
Something small is left behind
A ripple
Folding neatly
Across the water's line

And it folds into the ocean
Where it grows into a wave
Building in momentum
Strong and tall and brave

and we thank the wind for its whisper
Its gentle nudge this way
For all that it carried
For love that always stays

Yes we thank the wind for its whisper
For the love it gave
A love that we'll carry
Every day

FALLING THROUGH THE BLUE/GREY
SARA WEST

A rough looking girl, ripped sleeveless denim, black skinny's, beanie and boots sits on a mound of dirt. She stirs up the dust before she decides to speak. Her fist unconsciously clenched throughout—This is GREM

GREM

The water was crazy clear…

(*Beat*)

My dad used to work down here. Back when there was work and the dust wasn't empty the way it is now. The smallest breeze and you're covered in a haze of blue/grey shit you know you shouldn't be breathing in.

Anyway… dad's gone and the quarry's flooded now but completely beautiful… Since it closed down and the fluros hussled out the rain's been slowly seeping in to fill the fucking thing up. Bit by bit the quarry is taking back what we dug out… It's pretty great.

(GREM *jumps up suddenly, looks across the water and over the ridge as though she's heard something. Eventually she settles*.)

Anyway—that's how I know about this place. That's why we came camping here.

Hannah drove and I shot-gunned so Smith, Adelaide and Ebony shared the back with Theo, Hannahs brother. He didn't really have a seat or anything and he kept putting his feet in Smiths face. It was pretty funny cause she's rough as and hates kids. Ebony just read her book the whole way. Adelaide is a dumb cunt but funny as and I've been friends with her for ages so she had to come. (*laughing*) She squatted roadside on the way down and shit all over her jeans so she spent the whole week in her underwear…

(*Her laugh slowly fades out as she looks at her clenched fist—then.*)

Don't you think this place is incredible? It's kinda weird the way they just left it behind. Like suddenly nothing down here mattered as much as what was on the surface.

Me an' dad would spiral down to ground level in this fuck off truck that could probably crush a house if we wanted it too. I had to sit in the transportables pretty much all day but I'd get to put on a hard hat if I had to go to the toilet block for a piss. I'd step out into the blue/grey dust with dad's old work boots and sink a good two inches before I hit solid ground.

We got here Tuesday and by Friday night we were all pretty wrecked. We went swimming everyday and laughed at Adelaide when we found skiddys on her undies— she couldn't hide them without her jeans. Smith tried to show Theo how to kick the footy but his legs were too small and he was pretty unco so she got pissed off and went on hikes. Ebony kept reading her fucking books and it was dinner time before Hannah realised Theo was gone. One second he was a five-year-old on an adventure… another minute passed and he was missing…

We looked for him for ages but it was dark as and there was no way we were gunna find him… we kept searching… hunting for him in the night. By morning we were exhausted… and that's when we found him…

(*She stands on the mound and looks to something in the distance. A plume of dust is rising above the ridge—a car approaches.*)

That plume of dust? That's them… They're coming for me.

Ebony got there first. I guess she didn't really know how to react so she kind of casually called us over and was like 'Hey guys—I found Theo'. She kind of made it sound like he was okay? Like it had all been some stupid joke that went on for way to long but… nah…

Theo's body is all spazzy and his arm sticks out like a straw in a fruit box. He's bulky and solid but then one arm just comes out and twists towards the sky… like he made one last reach for the surface before he slid? He's wet himself at some point and there's a stack of flies hovering around his little body of broken bone. He's rolled down from the ledge one level up. It's about a thirty-foot fall and I guess… for a five-year-old… a deadly one.

Hannah is freaking out—she loses it completely. Smith kind of moves her to the side but she keeps trying to claw herself back closer to him. She's on her knees kicking up the dust before she gives into Smith and just cries and cries… cries for hours. Ebony stands over Theo for a little bit before she goes back to camp—probably to read a fucking book. Me and Adelaide stay with Theo… we probably stay too long… but I can't walk away. He holds me here with the blue/grey dust swirling at my feet and eventually the two of us… we're covered in it.

His little body… the blue/grey starts to build and he's already becoming part of the place… it didn't seem weird at the time.

(GREM *again distracted by the car approaching. A police siren maybe? It's close.*)

We didn't belong down here. Our tents and our sleeping bags; our fucking books and skiddy underwear; we weren't meant to be here, our shoes weren't meant to kick the dirt, we weren't meant to swim the waters or breathe this air but something about his broken body belonged to the quarry.

(GREM, *looking in the distance, slowly raises her hand directly out in front of her and slips a stream of blue/grey dust onto the floor while she speaks.*)

I pick up his little body… and he's was way lighter than I think he's gunna be so I stumble back a bit having braced myself for more weight. There's nothing in him anymore. Empty… like the dust. I take four solid steps towards the water's edge. I look out across the water, rippling in the wind, doing its best to fill a hole so fucking deep it can never be done… and I drop him. I drop him into the water.

The water's crazy clear down here… I watch his fruit box body spin awkwardly in the water and unravel through the crystal blue. A trail of blue/grey shit follows him down and he disappears into black

(*The dust in her hand runs out. The sirens are here.*)

They think I killed him… (*Beat*) I figure he's down on ground level… about where the toilet block used to be.

RED PANDA
AMANDA YEO

(*A museum. Asmara stands, looking at a portrait.*)

Mohammed said I remind him of a red panda.
I tell Lilah 'cause she thinks I'm smart and she says 'oh that's cute but.'
I tell her he thinks I'm dumb.
'No he doesn't.'
'Yeah he does. Pandas are dumb. They look like foxes only they're stupid. He thinks I'm pretty but stupid.'
'You're thinking about it too much.'
'He doesn't just say stuff like that okay? He thinks about it. He's thought about it.'
'Well, hey, at least he's thinking about you.'

We're trailing at the back of the class and Lilah's telling me about this guy she met at this party on Saturday. She says he's gorgeous and she reckons his lips could form strong enough suction to suspend him from a wall, but he's really hung up on Pluto not being a planet anymore, so. Mr Hancock yells at us to be quiet—well, not yells, museum yells. Yells like people yell when you're not supposed to yell. We ignore him. This excursion's boring. We're not even doing like, Asian studies or Asian art or whatever in class. Hancock's just got a hard on for stuff he finds exotic. First day of class I come in and he goes 'ni hao' and then just grins at me like I'm supposed to do something. So I say 'g'day mate' in the broadest Aussie accent I can muster and stare back at him the same way.

The exhibit's like twenty bucks, and that's just 'cause the school worked out some sort of package deal for the sixty of us. Otherwise it's forty-five bucks concession, which is like, a whole outfit if you're smart. It's stupid. I figure 'fuck it, I've paid my twenty bucks—I'm gonna get my money's worth'. Mr Hancock yells 'what did you just say, Asmara' and I say 'I said I love it, sir'.

So we walk in, and I'm helping Lilah weigh up the pros and cons of hooking up with Planetary Suction Man again, so I don't notice until we're standing right next to this display that they're the same plates we have at home.

Well, not the exact same plates, of course, but the same sort of plates—you know, the pink with the green phoenixes and whatnot? Up on shelves in the lounge. They're all bright like they were made by people who were super excited about discovering artificial colouring, but apparently they're really old.

'What's this?' I ask, 'cause the excursion letter just said 'temporary Asian exhibit'. Lilah gives me a pamphlet she picked up at reception 'cause she's a pamphlet klepto. It says 'Peranakans—come see this one time exhibition of antiques from a beautiful dying culture.'

Lilah's going 'This whole excursion's useless. Nobody's heard of these people. Hancock hasn't even mentioned Pear-anna-can art in class. It's not gonna be in the test'. Like she cares about the test. Art's a bludge subject anyway—that's the only reason anyone takes it. Art and drama. But her whining's getting on my nerves and I also think the guy's got a point about Pluto, so I act like I'm really interested in this plate and she gets bored and goes off to text Suction Man.

(*Pause.*)

There's this plate in the middle that's got flowers around the edge. It's kind of nice. It looks… it looks kind of exactly like that plate I smashed playing ball in the house when I was six. Mum told me not to play ball and I was only really playing ball 'cause she told me not to.

And in a glass case to the left there's the opium pipe that I stole from my grandma. I didn't steal it, I borrowed it. It's not stealing if you're family. I took the pipe from her place when I was seven because it's shaped like a rooster and it was pretty and shiny and she just put it on the shelf and didn't use it anyway. So I took it and used it to play farm.

There's a little plaque beneath it saying 'this is a Nyonya's opium pipe.'

Everything is laid out equal distances from each other with little descriptions. The shoes I ruined when I spilt paint on them. The brooch I broke the clasp off. The hairpin I took from my mum's dresser at home and used to poke holes in the dirt because I couldn't find a good enough stick.

It was like seeing my grandma's whole life reduced down to a pipe. My mum in a hair pin. Me in a plate. Laid out and labelled.

It's a proper museum and it's got the plate that I smashed when I was six.

I've basically paid twenty bucks to hang out in my grandma's house.

(*Pause. She looks around.*)

I can't find Mohammed. Can't hear Mr Hancock fake yelling at the class. Lilah's gone too. Everyone's moved on. Everyone's moved on and now it's just me and these things.

(*Pause.*)

It's like being at home, but in a lab. Everything's white and still and quiet. It's my past and it feels sterile. It feels like a museum. It's my family on display and I don't have anything. I have plates from Ikea and hair ties with plastic cartoon characters on them and thongs from the two dollar store.

I'm Mr Hancock. I'm a white Asian. I'm a red panda.

Mohammed's stopped looking at me. It's like he thinks he's better than me, like he knows he's better than me. My whole class is standing in my house looking at my things—my things that I know nothing about.

(*She looks at the portrait.*)

And then I see you. Brown and white and unsmiling. It's not like I've spent hours pouring over pictures of ancestors generations back. But I see your name. And I know that name. I know that name from all the times an aunt or uncle or cousin visited and my mum had to explain how we were related to them. And now you're sitting there in your rosewood chair, staring down at me the exact same way you stare down at everyone else. Staring down at me like you disapprove.

You're my family.

You're my great great grandfather.

You're mine.

(*Pause.*)

Mohammed will call me stupid. Lilah will call me stupid. You'd probably call me stupid too.

But the thing is, your descendants are dying. We're dying and there are monuments to us like we're already dead but nobody's trying to keep us alive. No one's trying to save us. We're not trying to save ourselves. We're just dying. And I don't want us to die. I don't want to die.

(*She reaches out toward the portrait as if to take it.*)

You're mine and no one will give you to me. Soon there's going to be nothing to give. And I'll just be… I'll just be… me.

And that's all. And that's it. We're dead.

(*Long pause. She retracts her hand.*)

I want it to feel like home.

And it doesn't.

AUTHOR BIOGRAPHIES

ARDA BARUT (*The Market Brolosopher*)

Arda Barut began his writing career early with his first poem and talent recognised at only thirteen years of age. He has been involved in writing/directing for theater early on in his artistic career. He co-directed and wrote a short work for UTP's Short'n'Sharp 3 in 2004 and worked as the director of photography and co-writer of the documentary Consumed in 2006. In 2009 Arda performed a live reading of his poems Bucket and The Sand Man at the Sydney Writers' Festival event Westside at the Wharf for the launch of the Westside New Series Volume 1: Fill Your Bucket publication. Arda has worked closely with Westside Publications to develop his strong literary background as a writer in Western Sydney. His writing reflects his determination to afford an authentic and literary voice to one of Australia's most misrepresented regions. Arda continues his work in poetry, photography and script writing and is eager to develop further outlets to express his artistic pursuits.

TANIA CAÑAS (*Untouchable*)

Tania has completed a Bachelor of Contemporary Arts (Drama and Psychology) and a Masters Degree in Communications at RMIT University. She has performed as part of the Melbourne Fringe Festival, Next Wave and Amnesty International's ARTillery Festival. Earlier this year Tania was selected for a PTO Scholarship to present at the 18th Annual Pedagogy and Theatre of the Oppressed Conference at the University of California, Berkeley. She presented her Masters Research findings in a presentation and subsequent Q&A panel session. Tania has provided communications support for events such as the Human Rights Arts & Film Festival, the Moon Lantern Festival and Wellbeing Festival. She has also stage-managed cultural events such as the Emerge Festival, Premiers Gala Dinner, Whitelion Bailout and Rhythm and Rights. Tania's was selected as an Emerging Cultural Leader by Footscray Community Arts Centre and currently works at Multicultural Arts Victoria and volunteers at RISE.

CHRISTOPHER HARLEY (*Birdcage*)

Christopher Harley is a Sydney-based writer and composer. With a focus in writing for theatre, Christopher's plays and musicals have been performed in Sydney and Newcastle, by both professional and co-operative companies. His first musical, *In a Pink Tutu*, was professionally premiered as part of the inaugural 2010 Sydney Fringe Festival with a successful season at the Seymour Centre. Before this, the musical was staged in Newcastle, winning him a City of Newcastle Dramatic Award. His theatre songs have been performed by renowned singers throughout Australia and his short plays *The 90-Second Party* and *Box* have been featured at Short+Sweet play festivals across Australia. Most recently he was won first place in atyp's ‹Love Bytes› national film-writing competition for his short film *How Was Work?* and his first full-length play *The Kimono-Wearing Queen* is currently undergoing professional development with Queensland Theatre Company and PlayLab Australia. Christopher also works as a freelance incidental music composer and has composed the scores for plays including *The Hour We Knew Nothing of Each Other*, *Woyzeck*, *A Midsummer Night's Dream* and *Love's Triumph*. Christopher holds a Bachelor of Music (Hons) from the Sydney Conservatorium of Music.

JULIA-ROSE LEWIS (*This Feral Life*)

Julia-Rose Lewis is a writer, performance maker and arts administrator currently working full time as The Youth Program Coordinator for Queensland Theatre Company. In 2010 Julia-Rose graduated with Distinction from QUT with a Bachelor of Creative Industries (Drama). Julia is passionate about writing for both the stage and screen. Most recently Julia was selected to attend ATYP's National Young Writer's Studio which saw the creation of a monologue titled *This Feral Life*. Julia's other theatre credits include; As Writer: *The Girl Who Fell In Love With Winter* (QUT Production 3, 2010), As Performer: *Elephant Gun* (The Escapists & BreadBeard Collective, World Theatre Festival 2011 and 2012), As Assistant Director: *GENESIS* by Benjamin Knapton (QUT, 2009), *The Tell Tale Heart* (QUT, 2009), As Dramaturg: *R&J >< Greater Than Less Than Ampersand Romeo And Juliet* (Vena Cava Productions, 2010) Other: Associate Artistic Director (Vena Cava Productions, 2010), Program Assistant (KITE Arts Education Program QPAC, 2010, 2011).

TOM MESKER (*The Mangroves*)

From Sydney's Northern Beaches, Tom Mesker is an actor, writer and director. Tom has acted from a young age and thinks this sparked his passion and interest in theatre and film, saying that each are like limbs. Honing his craft in Bathurst at CSU, in its Theatre and Media degree, Tom performed in and co-created many theatre projects and wrote and directed *Portraits*, a site specific theatre event as his major work project. Since then he has achieved a Certificate in Drama and Performing Arts through A.M.E.B, written *Spinning* that appeared in Melbourne's Short and Sweet festival and performed in multiple stage plays and short films. Tom has facilitated workshops in improvisation at Newtown High School through NYTC and also tutors drama to high school students with an emphasis on HSC performance development.

JOEL PERLGUT (*These Things Happen*)

Joel Perlgut is a dedicated follower and sometimes writer of theatre, film and fiction. He has written articles for *Time Out Sydney* and *UTS Vertigo*. His debut short film *The F***Up,* which he wrote and produced, is being rolled out to festivals early 2013. In his spare time he pretends to study Media Arts in Production at UTS.

CHARLES PURCELL (*Silo*)

Charles Purcell is a Sydney-based actor and writer. Since graduating from the University of Technology's creative writing program in 2011, Charles has taken part in the ArtStart Young Screenwriters' Program at Metro Screen, participated in atyp's Fresh Ink National Studio, and undertaken a dramaturgy internship with PlayWriting Australia under the mentorship of Chris Mead. In 2012 Charles wrote and performed work for Shopfront Contemporary Arts and Performance, Griffin Theatre Company's Griffringe, and Tamarama Rock Surfers' Cut & Paste. He is a member of performance ensemble piLAB, and co-founded independent company Starving Wolf with which he was a recent resident of The Rocks Pop-Up Artists' Initiative. Most recently Charles worked as actor and dramaturg on Tim Spencer's *Show Me Yours, I'll Show You Mine*, winner of the Innovation in Theatre award and award for Best Performance in the 2012 Melbourne Fringe Festival.

IZZY ROBERTS-ORR (*Peach*)

Izzy Roberts-Orr is 21 and really tall for her age. She lives in Brunswick, Melbourne in a house with lots of records, never enough clothes and too many stairs. Izzy writes poems and sometimes speaks them through microphones because it's fun to see what people will do when you throw words at them. Izzy writes plays (*NightMinds, Twins*) and sometimes people act them in front of audiences (Adelaide Fringe, MKA at MTC). Izzy Roberts-Orr talks back.

RANDA SAYED (*Private Research*)

Randa is an actor, writer and director from Western Sydney. She studied performance at the University of Western Sydney, Jacques Lecoq School of Movement and Theatre & Zen Zen Zo. Her recent acting credits include her self-devised piece *Experience and the Girl* 2nd Griffringe 2012 and *Heart Dot Com*. She performed her writing as part of BYDS 2012 Sydney Writers' Festival event, *Moving People*. *Westside New Series: Vol. 2* was her first appearance in a literary journal. Her directing credits of 2012 include the Young Creative Festival of Shorts and the short film: *Dead Boy*. Her entry into atyp's *Love Bytes* competition, *Loaded*, was shortlisted and shown as part of the Colourfest film festival in Sydney. In 2012 she worked closely with BYDS and STC on the production *Look The Other Way* and is directed a performance as part of PYT's 25th Birthday Celebration.

KRYSTAL SWEEDMAN (*Sunrise Set*)

Krystal is a Brisbane-based creative. Since completing a drama degree at the University of Queensland she has immersed herself in the world of theatre; watching productions, devouring scripts and exploring the theatrical possibilities of the written word. She recently took part in atyp's National Studio '12 and was selected to receive development on her script *Crema* through Queensland Theatre Company's Young Playwright Program in 2012. Earlier in the 2012 her monologue *Babycino* was performed during Anywhere Theatre Festival. Other playwriting credits include *The Green Bag Bandits*, a short play produced by Underground Productions and lyrics for the musical; *Tribes of Avalon*. She has also dabbled in sound design, is currently writing, directing and producing a documentary on the making of Monster's Appear *A Tribute of Sorts* and was an intern at Playwriting Australia's 2010 National Play Festival in Sydney.

SARA WEST (*Falling Through the Blue/Grey*)

Having studied in Adelaide and moved interstate, Sara is a Sydney-based actor and aspiring writer... she babysits two kids and works in a fish and chip shop. With interests in all sides of filmmaking she hopes to produce screenplays with strong female characters and a unique Australian voice. Currently in post-production of her short film, *River Water*; which she wrote and directed, Sara hopes to be working on feature length content very soon. Alongside her independent ambitions as a writer Sara is also going into production on a feature film called *One Eyed Girl* and has recently been seen in *Babyteeth* at Belvoir St Theatre [2012]. In 2013 she will appear in *Dreams in White* at the Griffin Theatre Company [2013].

AMANDA YEO (*Red Panda*)

Amanda Yeo is a playwright, author, and pop culture enthusiast. Currently studying BA Communication (Writing and Cultural Studies)/ B Laws at UTS, she is still growing up in Western Sydney and has been writing for as long as she can remember—so since about 1994. She had her first play performed at Short and Sweet when she was 16, and since then has performed her work at 2012 Sydney Writer's Festival event Moving People, Bankstown's 2011 Youth Week event Own It!, and on FBI Radio's All the Best segment. She has also been published in the *Tiny Book of Tiny Stories: Vol 1*, *UTS Writers' Anthology 2011: The Life You Chose and that Chose You*, and *Westside New Series Vol 2: On Western Sydney*. Amanda enjoys comic books, action movies, and video games, and is embarrassed by rude words.

www.currency.com.au

Visit Currency Press' website now to:

- Buy your books online
- Browse through our full list of titles, from plays to screenplays, books on theatre, film and music, and more
- Choose a play for your school or amateur performance group by cast size and gender
- Obtain information about performance rights
- Find out about theatre productions and other performing arts news across Australia
- For students, read our study guides
- For teachers, access syllabus and other relevant information
- Sign up for our email newsletter

The performing arts publisher